The poetry here comes from the depths of my heart I have so far dived into and recovered in my life. A vortex of words and emotions hidden except to me. My own vault of inspiration and chaos. A void, a receiver box for the echoes of God and the lost inner child. A lion. Hear me roar.

Chapter 1:

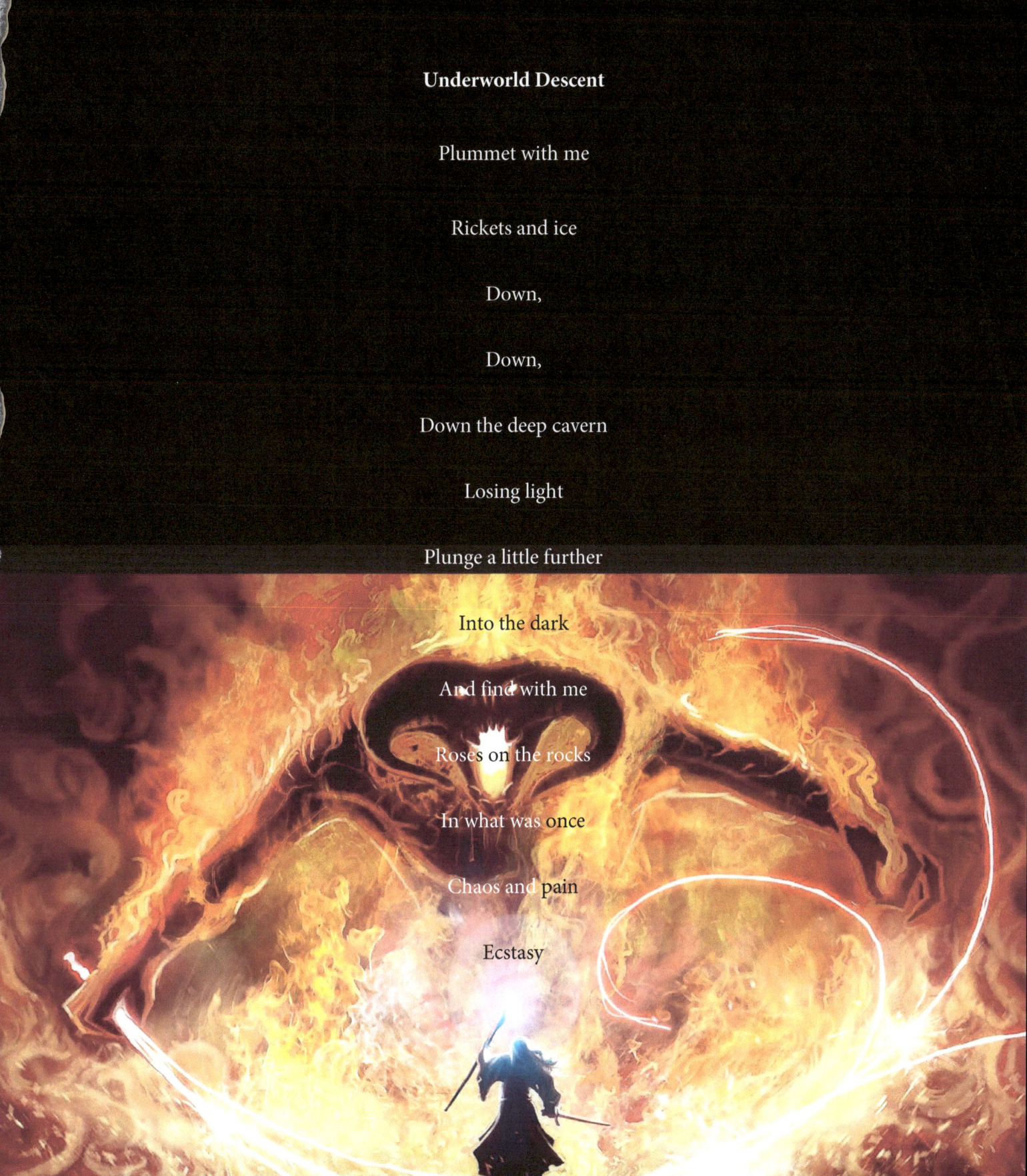

Underworld Descent

Plummet with me

Rickets and ice

Down,

Down,

Down the deep cavern

Losing light

Plunge a little further

Into the dark

And find with me

Roses on the rocks

In what was once

Chaos and pain

Ecstasy

Born in Darkness

I fucking love the darkness and pain

I let it melt my flesh

Shred my brain

Open my vein

Drink my sweet blood

And moan that life is miserable and sweet

Thank you for letting me love you

And becoming my best friend

My old self merely adopted the darkness

I was born in it.

A Choked Flower Bud

I see the thread

Of a pained hunched constipated body

Riveted mind, eyes dashing anxiously

Amassing indexes of information

Assuaging the institutional data quota

Surviving through a psychic slog

Brain and jaws clenched

Leaving his laptop,

Laying on the mattress

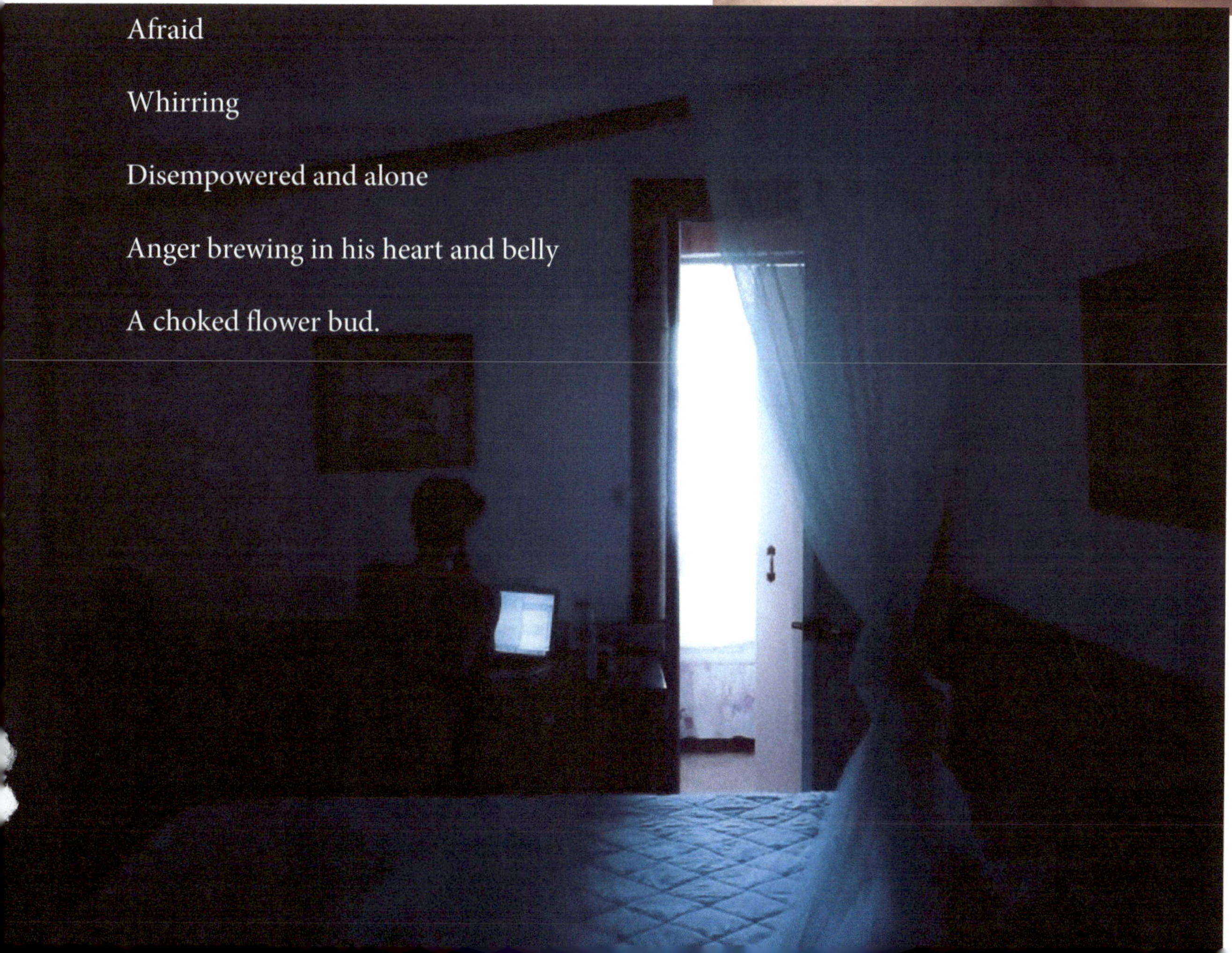

Afraid

Whirring

Disempowered and alone

Anger brewing in his heart and belly

A choked flower bud.

Dark Mother

You crush me
With naked, fibrous vines
In the depth of your teeming womb
the darkness floods
I let it drown me

Flooded by dreams of Nature's vast bosom
I rest in the bathtub,
There's no light
Just a tender belly
And you, Dark Mother
Suffocating me with life

Dark Mother, what I see churns within
the frightening force of yin

Turning the world
Like an elemental hologram
Feasting on light
Like my pale skin

Dark Mother moansand listens
Soothing the primal fibers
Of a lost child
Frozen and malnourished
Over the ages,
Lost in the wild
Tremblingly clutching a steel cord of destruction
But brimming with Dark Mother's
Angry, wild poetry.

Pain

A hard raft

In a flaming ocean

Pain

Reminds me

I'm alive

And still have

So much to learn

Pain

Is my teacher

Showing me the

Hidden path

Into the back alleys,

Deep crags,

Otherwise alien glints of my soul

Pain

Makes me want to run

In despair

But somehow,

I breathe.

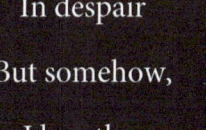

Inner Mordor

The air here reeks of death

And impending bloodshed

Not a flower blooms

A pestilent fume

Leaks out of the infected womb

A screech

A warped roar

Eschewing touch for the kiss of death

Crying in a tongue alien to love

If you wander too close to this forsaken realm

Gollum will lure you

Lead you on an endless labyrinth

And distract you from the ghostly black knife

Clutched by a hand of reptilian scales and metal

Patiently dangling above your supple organs

Falling with a final bout

Of liberating, all-effacing fury

I see blood and screeching

Before slipping back

Into my dark, void mother

Cursing numb immature men

As I join the undead race of them.

Dark Mother Part II

Dark Mother's vines linger

Over concrete urban phalluses

Her veins of cellulose paw

At the rims of order and society

In me, she hisses

Who are you feeding,

My spawn of decomposition

Or me, in your self?

Dark Mother, I listen

My heart burns

I'm coming to my knees

Naked, wet,

A modern man dismembered

As much as I slash at your arms

And rip and till your breasts

I long to be cradled in your teeming bosom

To roar in our sacred bond

Drown me in your greatness.

Martyr Mystic

Life rips me apart

Again and again

Just when the hope

That I could be happy

Tickles my childisb heart

Tbe pit of nothingness

I WAS SPECIAL!

Sucks me in

And I,

Flooded by memories
NOOOOO!
Drown beneath my dreams
ok.

Beauty in my Broken Reflection

I run from pain,

Truth,

And blame.

I run from

A heart

Breathless womb.

I run from light

Because darkness

Lets me go invisible.

I run from

Life, but cling to

Its forms and familiarity

Because if I don't

I'm afraid

I'll be a crazy sad lonely nobody

And have missed something.

No God,

I cannot but be you

Beauty in my broken reflection.

Rebirth

Birth is when

The lights

Down every corridor

Of conscious possibility close

And I cannot breathe

I hold my throat a moment longer It

feels like dying

Do I surrender?

Or BREATHE

The holy vapor around me

Tear my away from the dark canopy

And see my fingers,

Caressing the carpet

The floor holds me

A lonely child,

His own prophet, worst enemy

And natural entity

Writing poetry just to be seen

How can we truly connect and see

When these words say so little

And entire cosmos lay between?

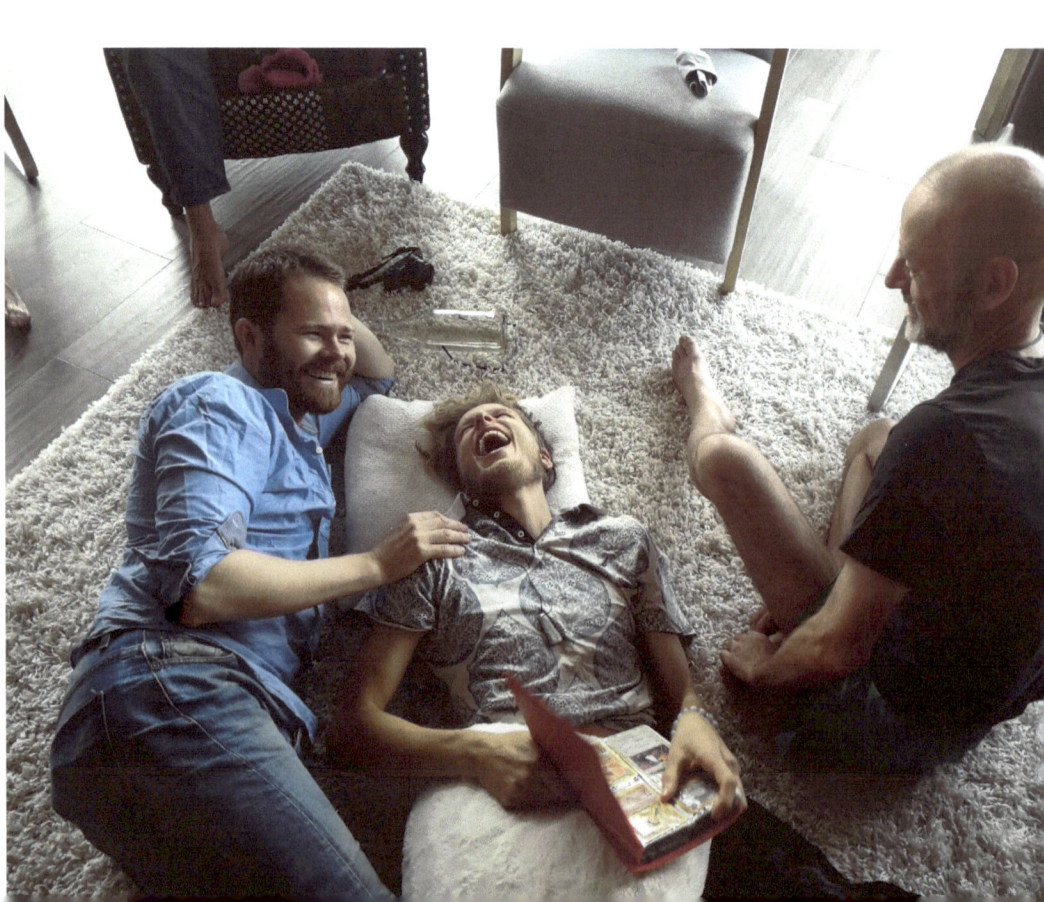

The Journey of Self Love

So you feel the unbearable squeal

Slowly winding its way through your nerves

And all you can do

Is shake, grab a cookie

Turn on a movie

And half feel

You are still there

The cord of love

Swings in the ether

Still

You are always there

As that squeal

Quietly awaits your self love.

Chapter 2: Whispers

Soul Water

Maybe I'm just
An empty cup
Blossoming
For God to fill me up
And quench
My brothers and sisters thirst
Soul water
Here brxthers and sxsters

I have a little cup.

God

I came here

Walked outside the womb

Lights and groans

Nervous ticks I took on

From too much time alone

I wandered so long

That I lost the way home

My tracks on the sand

Washed to sea

Alone at the lighthouse

Looking out at a vast strange world

Afraid to die,

Afraid to live

I curled up

Hoping you'd come

Hold me

After a long time

No one came

Until finally I realized

You were always holding me

Because you are me

And I love me

All my toes,

My heart and guts

We wrap up

A wet wailing bundle of being

The only good thing

That has ever come to me

Thank you God.

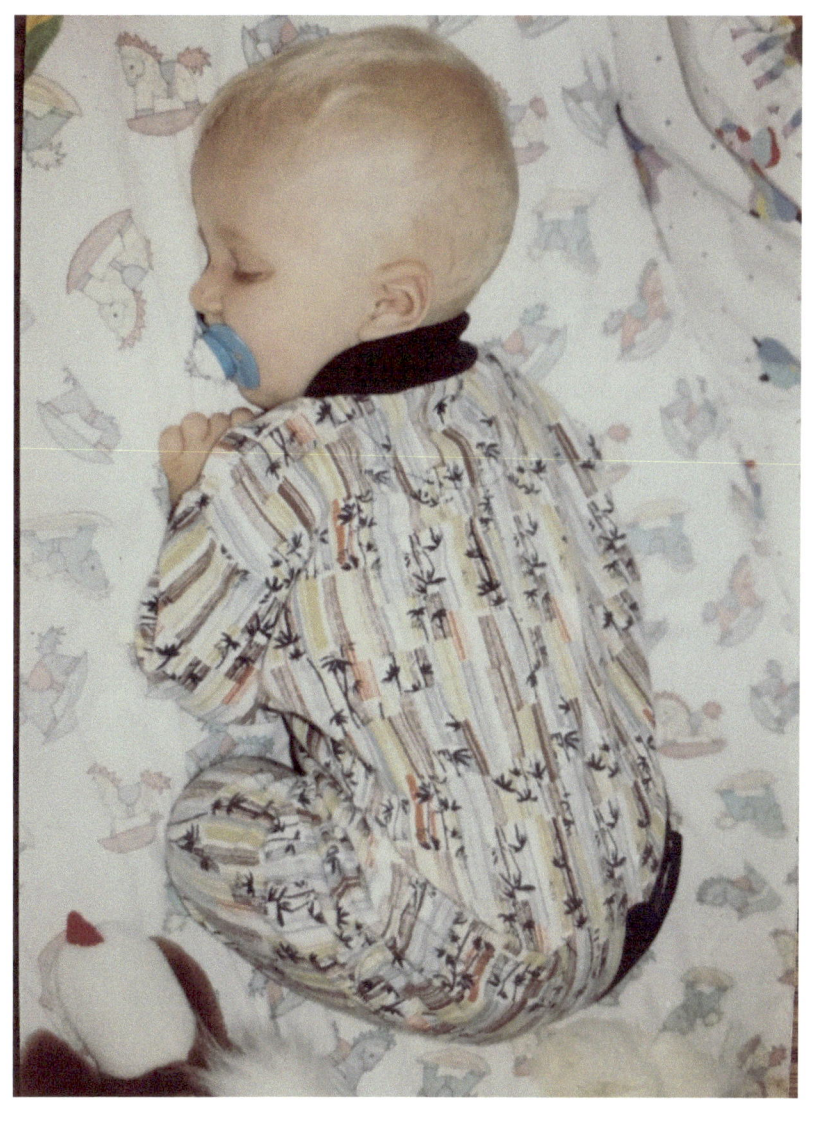

Dear Pattie

I love you

I miss you so much

You were a mother to me

And best friend

You showed me light

Where all I would've known is fear

You brought me to the gates of heaven

With the simple truths

Of being kind and sincere

You roused my spirit when I felt alone

Your spirit persists in me

Forever, to my very bones

I love you

And miss you dearly

I know you hear me

Hallelujah.

Dear Mom and Dad,

    For all the family dinners, however awkward they may have been, for all the Christmas presents Mom mostly wrapped and labeled (sometimes from the enigmatic Santa), taking us snowboarding even when you had no interest in braving ice and inexperience, for the vacations spent on the cool lakes of Minnesota where I found a passion for exploring tiny lichen-laden rock islands and flame fried walleye, for paying for my long flights and journeys to other far away countries where you hardly knew what your child was doing and experiencing, for bringing me to Shakespeare plays to experience the raw sweaty passion and hilarity of intimate live shows that I'd otherwise pass over for long nights of video games, for nurturing me from a little fetus to a grown man, for going to my graduations, for hosting my birthday parties and honoring my requests to have Michael Jordan fill in for "Evan", for birthday candles, cards, wishes, and family time, for showing kindness to Pattie, for beach days at Point Pleasant, for long walks in cold local parks, `(for the unconcious pain, fear, and demons that have forced me to grow)`,

                              for life.

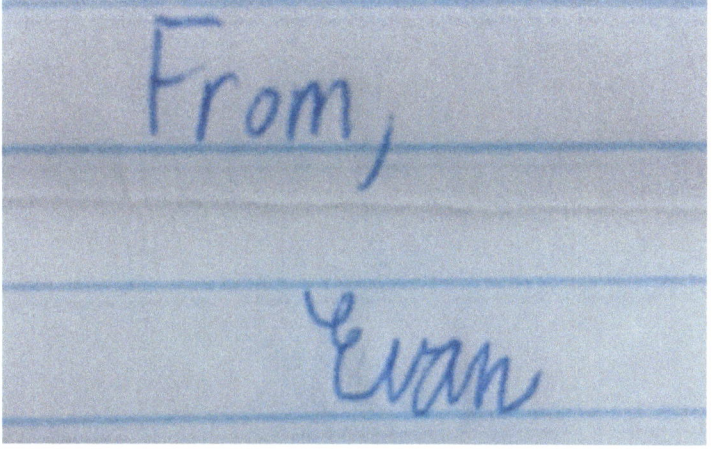

The truth is

I have unconsciously created

Much of

If not

All of

My own suffering

I am sorry
Please forgive me
Thank you
I love you.

Rain

Reminds me

Of the falling kites

Joyful nights

Spent breathing with myself

At peace with being

In love with aloneness

Those nights

Discovering myself in silence

Earthling

Plants squished beneath my toes
Fear fountaining out my chest
A splay of stars
Wreath the realm above
I hear chirping
A heart that beats
I try to breathe but it only travels so far
Things contract around my natal star
Dragons swoosh and I ripple too
Millions of people in my mind's view
Yet I'm just here, with a couple of trees
I am here, somehow healthy
Somehow, free

A force pushes me down,
I owe my life to you
Grand Force, Oneness, Being,
I am being enough,
Being is enough

Yet I feel alone,
Blind to the woody fingers
Springing towards me,
Seeking another being
To touch and say
I am here, we are brothers of the earth
Since a cosmic candle
First lit the horizon's hearth

Infinite Roots

Rich swinging pines
Sap spilling down its vines
Leaves bristle
Remembering winter
Falling whispers
Patting hard earth

I'm seeking
The wind blows harder
It's cold
Every moment

Breathe

There's just a tree in the breeze
With roots in infinity.

The Garden

Sometimes needs watering
Sometimes,
Its leaves grow mold
Sometimes,
Its soil's depleted
Sometimes,
Sunlight's needed

I was once told
I should forget about this garden
And let it grow old

Still,
I water, wash, and hold

This gift
And cross
Nature's
Subtle, sacred
Multiorganismic symphony.

Ayahuasca

Your vine

Coiled down my spine

You brought me to my knees

And in agony

For the first time

Ever

I genuinely

Prayed to God.

Stars

God loves being us
So grateful
To have known every last
Speck of fear and dust
We bore

See our spacetime canvass
Ripping at the seams
Earth contorting
Into a a distant glow.

I now know
There has never been anything
But what is,
And what is can only be
Loved

We're dying and flickering
What is   a   human!?
\\
Message over.

I love life
All these messages
Are for
When I'm dead
So that you remember
That I said
I love life

Dying Questions

Have you spoken those words

From the tip of your known

Have you seeped wider

Into the ocean of the unknown?

Gates

There comes a time
During the day
When, with a crack,
Infinity opens
And I,
In terror,
Gawk at the gates.

Terror

Wipes my memory

Seals the vault to

Everything

Left in the abyss

No left,

No right

Just this

Trembling body

In mist.

Ceremony Sin Ceso

Breathe

Everything is growing

Morphing

Dying

Breathe

You've been here before

All along

Ride now,

Stay still

This is the way things are

Until they're not

Change

Even if

The lights of heaven

Are robbed

And my body

Is sick and

In chains

There is a place inside me

That knows

Everything changes

And that this refuge

Can never die.

The present is a single point.

The past is a vicious ocean ready to suck you into the depths of the unresolved emotion and pain of one of your millions of lonely, impatient inner children with a single wave.

The future is a mirage on the horizon stranding you in the depths of murky, false self-prophecy.

Now is a raft guiding you to the grey havens of infinity. Right now there is no you. The world is nothing.

And everything is born anew.

Madre

Thank you.

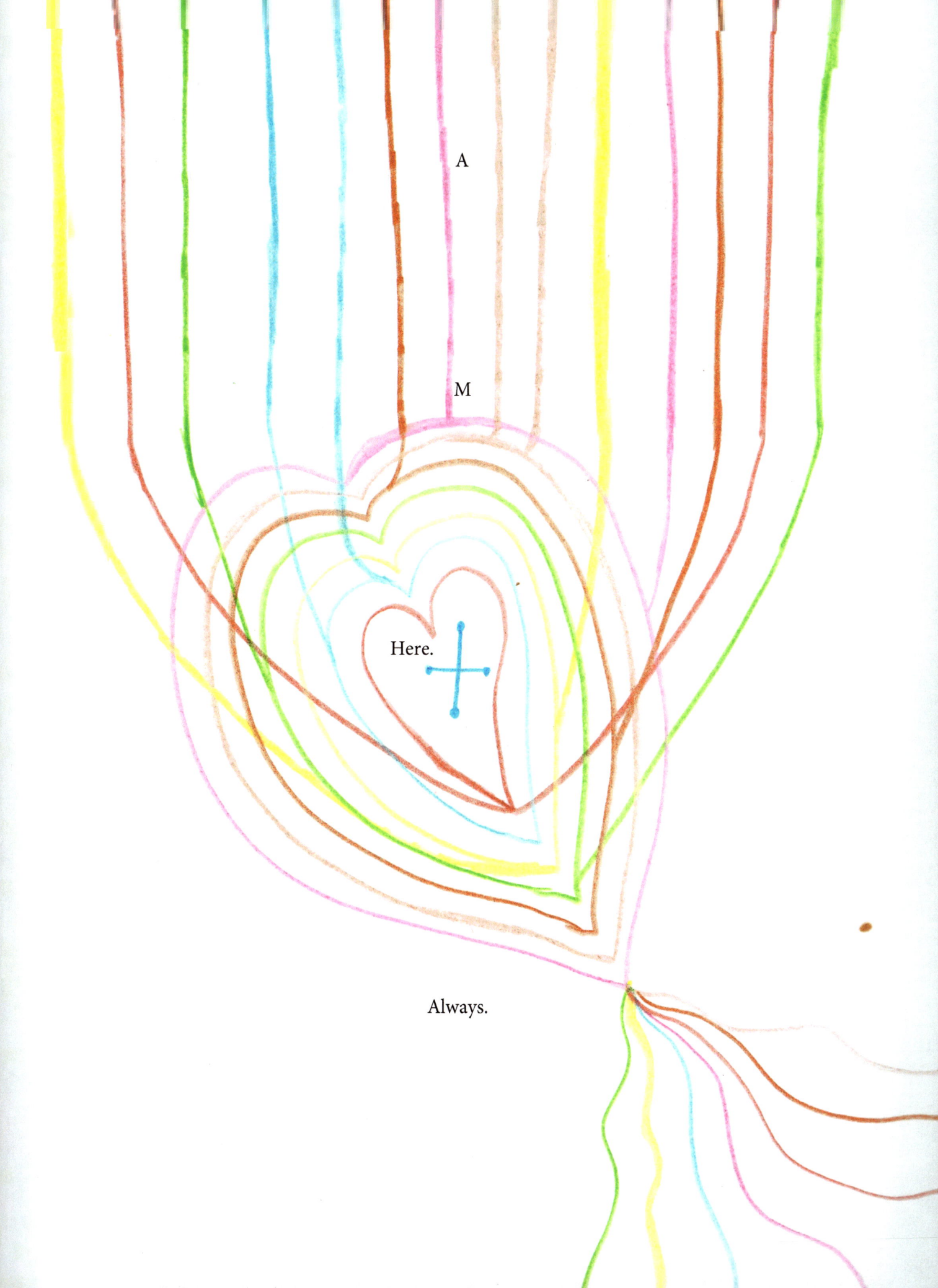

Words for the Weary

There is no need to be afraid
Fear reminds us
Of Life's preciousness
It's an opportunity
To come alive
And humbly, gently,
Courageously
Embrace our craziness.

Ong Namo

The rain is pouring down
Like all the souls you sent here
Coming to this earth
To find healing

Mother earth takes in the rain
Like your heart takes my voice
Let us free each other
With our prayers, with our voice.

-Snatam Kaur

Thank you to all my teachers, guides, and friends.

Citation

Page 1: NASA's Goddard Space Flight Center

Page 2: Martin Pugh, Heaven's Mirror Observatory

Page 4: Entroz of DevianArt, also known as Space Gooose on Instagram

Page 6, 12, 25: Emiliano Zuñigah Hernandez

Page 25: Left image - Optical: ESO/VLT; Close-up - X-ray: NASA/CXC/Curtin University/R.Soria et al., Optical: NASA/STScI/Middlebury College/F.Winkler et al